ARRIVAL PRESS

TWO by TWO

Edited by Tim Sharp

TWO by TWO

Edited by Tim Sharp

First published in Great Britain in 1997 by

A R R I V A L   P R E S S
1-2 Wainman Road, Woodston,
Peterborough, PE2 7BU
Telephone (01733) 230762

HB ISBN 1 85786 631 2
SB ISBN 1 85786 626 6

Foreword

Britain is a nation of animal lovers; a pet to us is more than just an animal, they're part of the family.

Two by Two is inspired by animals and their behaviour, the poems reflect the owners' thoughts, feelings and emotions about their pets, past and present.

This anthology is entirely dedicated to animals, and conveys the message that animals really are 'Man's Best Friend'.

I hope you enjoy reading this as much as I did whilst editing it.

Tim Sharp
Editor

Contents

The Poems

Absent Friends

(Dedicated to the cat next door 'Pusskins')

Kiss my world away - they are taking my lodger away.
Far away to another land,
To where there is, plenty of sand.
Blue sky overhead - blue sea all around,
What is the name of this foreign land?
Spain - so far away.
No more cuddles; day after day.
No rolled up paper - you chasing it about,
Till in the end - you are worn out.
You lying over my glossy mags,
Pieces of string - telephone cable,
All have a tug - that's of course, when you feel able.
There you are chasing about
Who' going to chase my spiders out.
No more claws in my carpets and chairs;
None of those loose black and white hairs.
Your blue comb lying there - looking at me
Saying I wonder - where she can be,
Your daily groom - is a part of me.
Your empty dishes put away
If only your owners - would let you stay;
Seven years - we have shared together
We are friends forever and ever.
And, I know you won't like - that hot Spanish weather.
So many hours - we share throughout the day
How do I live - in these nightmare days!
Without your love day after day.
No words can express - my breaking heart
With so much distance - we are worlds apart.

Margaret J Franklin

I Wanted A Chimp

I fell in love at the zoo one day,
With a baby chimpanzee as he smiled my way.
I'd like to take him home for my own pet,
But I didn't realise what I was to get.

With his big brown eyes and button nose,
A lovely smile and a natural pose,
Big long arms nearly touching the floor
I didn't know he would swing on my door.

Bouncing hard upon my chair,
I hope they do not tear,
Hanging on curtains, swinging on poles,
But he doesn't do as he is told.

Emptying cupboards throwing everywhere
He just laughed and couldn't care.
Climbing the stairs and sliding down,
Until bump as he hits the ground.

Diving into my big bed,
Doesn't he listen to what I've said,
Roly poly and handstands too,
What am I going to do.

Pulling my sheets having pillow-fights,
When does he sleep it's nearly midnight,
The very next day I call the zoo,
Hurry up and make it soon.

With a hairy hug and a sloppy kiss,
This is what I shall miss
Behind the bars, on a branch he climbs
This is the best place for him to be,
And he is not at all missing me.

Christine Kowalkowski

McCartney

He came to me second-hand,
Underweight, semi-wild - not very grand.

A few years later, things are not the same,
He's now well fed, very spoilt, he even likes a game!

His name is McCartney, he is a real friend to me,
A big ginger cat, near to me he wants to be.

I am glad he came my way, maybe fate played a hand,
To help him discover my little plot of land!

Patricia Thomas

My Queen

The Queen she sits before the fire
In her golden coat attired;
Each little paw strategically placed,
Each little hair to be licked in place!
Toes to be widened,
Claws to be trimmed,
Tail to be smoothed, to the tip of its brim!
Ears to be washed,
Whiskers preened,
Oh what a job
Has my little Queen!

Barbara Crook

Cadbury - My Pelican

My flat is very small
Four metres from wall to wall
Scarcely room to hang a hat
Let alone swing a cat
But I have a pelican - who - what's more
Lays chocolate cream eggs by the score

My fashionable fowl (from fun fur stock)
Needs no exercising walk
His food intake's exactly nil
And I've yet to foot a veterinary bill
From the ceiling he takes view
Thro' two button eyes of blue

Children when they come to tea
Say 'Please will you lay an egg for me!'
And gasp - when magically - chocolate cream eggs
Appear from behind short spindly legs
As I bungee him up an' down
From 'springy-bobs' hooked to his crown

Cadbury means the world to me
He's delightful company
Doesn't flap when I holiday
Looks after himself whilst I'm away
Today he's making his debut
To introduce himself to you

Anna MacDonald

Pip

Such a tiny ball
Of apricot fur.
Such a long tail
Wrapped round it all.
Two eyes as bright
As glistening dew.
Dear Pip the hamster
This was you.

Transferring the food
Filling your pouches
Soft white bedding
Kept on the move.
You'd disappear
Vanish from view.
Dear Pip the hamster
We'd find you.

Stopping for a groom
Behind tiny ears.
Quick as a flash
Around the room.
You were such fun,
Intelligent too.
Dear Pip the hamster
We miss you.

May Purves

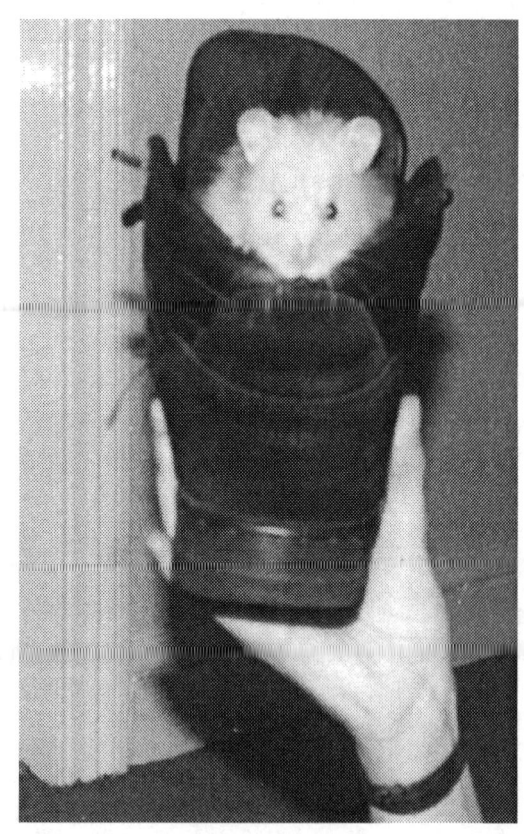

Beauty Without Cruelty

If you desire a beautiful face
Smooth, lovely and full of grace
Don't be cruel to God's animal creatures
They were not meant to improve human features.

Try herbs and flowers of the field
Skin and hair will bloom and yield
Animal lovers get true beauty this way
Ring the Lady Dowding's boutique right away.

Scorn a coat made of skin or fur
Think of the animal, the pain you incur
A seal skin coat may last for years
But think of the bloodshed, pain and tears.

Innocent seal pups don't do any harm
Don't depend on a bludgeoned pup to keep you warm
A good impression fur looks really just as nice
And an innocent animal's life didn't pay the price.

Animals feel fear, heartbreak, pain
Like humans they see the sun and the rain
Let every spiritual soul take the lead and pray
That beauty without cruelty may come to stay.

D Bowden

Our Little Sue

A dumpy frame on stumpy legs
Holds one out whene'er she begs
Our little Sue as she was known
Into a lovely bitch she'd grown
She was a sexy little critter
Always seemed to have a litter
Puppies would come by the score
When they went, she'd have more
With us in our loving home
One of our family she'd become
With our kiddies she would play
Guarding them in every way
But that fateful day she died
We all sat around and cried
In our garden I dug her grave
For the love to us she gave
To us her memory will never fade
As in her grave she's gently laid
But now we know her pain will cease
In God's place where she's at peace.

David Brownley

The Fledgling

With tiger eyes, and claws so bright,
And sharp fangs gleaming in the light,
In stole the cat, purring loudly,
And gladly at my feet let fall
A fluffy ball which squeaked and bled;
And which wriggled and squealed and swayed.
It was bedraggled and afraid.
Recovering from its dreadful fright,
It tried hard to hide out of sight.
I picked it up in my cupped hands.
It nestled down in the slight warmth.
Then it sat up and cried and cried
For food; for food to be supplied.
I had committed a foul sin.
It turned cold with eyes sunken in,
And for as long as I shall live
I shall remember the cherub
With its claws and downy feathers.

Doreen King

Little And Large!

Little cat has become large cat!
I fear I'm chiefly to blame.
She comes each day for her breakfast.
The ritual is always the same.

As soon as I put the hall light on
I know she's waiting there,
demanding that I let her in,
so, because it's only fair

to neighbours still asleep, I do!
Then comes the loving part:
she pushes her nose into my face
and nestles against my heart.

Her fur is often cold or wet
but it has to be massaged well,
down to the very tip of her tail;
I love it, truth to tell.

Then the business part of the visit:
a run to the waiting tray
where she always finds some goodies,
different every day.

She wants to come into the house, though,
from the garage where I feed her;
turning her out is not easy.
Sometimes I have to lead her

I'd love to keep this beauty
and I know she's longing to stay,
but, alas, she doesn't belong to me,
so I send her on her way.

Geraldine Squires

The Dolphins

Tossed on the foaming waves of night
We sailed through cloaking darkness
Dense as tarry pitch
The gale subsiding with the hours
Until by dawn came grateful calm
And with it came the dolphins.
A graceful escort for a wearied crew
The sea alive with swift and leaping forms
As young and caring old swam side by side
Dark silhouettes all caught by rising sun
Its golden path spread wide across the water.
The rigours of a storm tossed night now passed
They brought delight and sparking life
To sleepless brains.

Carol Rickard

Angie (My Stick Insect)

Her home is just a large glass jar
And so she doesn't wander far
But once a day I take her out
So she can have a walk about
Excited to be really free
She crawls upon my stockinged knee.
Though not outside to cling on trees
She sways as in a dancing breeze
She simulates a twig so well
The difference you cannot tell.
Although she's slender as a pin
From time to time she sheds her skin
(A lot of people do not know
But this is how these insects grow)
Angie's lifespan's but a year
And when she goes I'll shed a tear.

Mary Rea

After 'Tramp' ... 'Sweep' ...

Tramp is a hard act to follow,
looking back, he was all that a dog should be.
Fluffy and black, found as a stray
he gambolled, he slept, and he smiled at me.
At the end of our tears, at our parting,
we walked through kennels, to find
two hundred homeless, none of them Tramp,
so we left the barking behind.
We thought of names, for an elegant breed.
Barnaby, Rowan? . . . Too soon
fate led us to Sweep, another in need.
Leggy and boisterous,
sprinkling of spaniel
with a brown spot
where a spot shouldn't be.
Due to be put down the following day
offered, (on trial), what could we say?
He chases the cats, stealing the meat,
digs up the garden, then lays on our feet.
Resentful, they fed him, awaiting the time, when
they could reject him, turn him loose.
Forgiving? Forgetting? He loves all the children,
Time is our healer, for better or worse.

Bobbie Dee

Bess And Vanilla

(In memory 1978-1994)

I got them for a present,
One all black and one all white.
They were so very tiny
I let them sleep with me first night,
Next day they wandered round the house,
To find their way about.
With doors and windows tightly closed,
In case one of them got out.
When they got a little older,
I let them venture to outside.
They loved it in the garden,
They would play and they would hide.
But when they grew much older
They both went their separate ways.
The white one she moved upstairs,
And lived there night and day,
The black one she stayed downstairs,
When I sat, was by my side.
Unless she found a box or bag,
She would jump in to play and hide.
Twice a day they both did meet,
When I put out their food for them to eat.
Sometimes the white one downstairs would stay,
And with the black one, they would play.
But still was there when I went up to bed,
And slept on my pillow above my head.
I had them both for many years,
And in their passing shed many tears.

J M James

What To Call A Cat

Socrates is his full name
'Tho *Sox* or *Socket* is what I claim
his name to be when he is here.
Let me make that crystal clear.

What he calls himself? Who knows,
completely different I suppose.
Sometimes I call him worse than that
when I chastise my tabby cat.

For up the curtain he'll ascend.
(It really drives me round the bend)
So *little brat's* a favourite quote.
But I don't mean it, please take note.

And if I call him will he come?
Not on your life, his nose he'll thumb
unless it's food, my brindled sinner,
don't call *him* too late for his dinner!

A E Abbott

To My Faithful Dog Rex

(Died 23rd March 1985)

Night and day
I stand awake,
remembering
your quiet breath;

But it's not there
you are gone,
forever
to another world;

You departed
wagging your tail,
gazed
with melting eyes;

Even though
I took you to
die,
I'll never forget;

Now here I stand
your collar in my hand,
thinking
of my long lost friend.

Raymond Fenech

Gentle Friend

Five years now passed
since you were so downcast
All that suffering, misery and pain
replaced with loving care again

Always am I in your sight
with you tight upon my heels
Wherever I decide to go
you must always be there too!

Flies and wasps
make you incredibly cross
Snapping and biting
Inevitably a sting
a huge cry will it bring

But you never complained
when granddaughter Zoe
Opened your mouth to examine your teeth
then lifted your ears in sheer disbelief

Pepper, gentle little friend
bringing to us so much joy
And never-ending loyalty,
rarely ever found in man!

Gail Crumpton

Little Man

A little man has come to stay, his coat is black and white.
He's made our comfy home his own. He's a very welcome sight.
The kitchen door's been made his size, with a flap, for in and out.
All his freedom's still his own, as he wanders all about.

We'll be sitting in the evening - the telly on to watch.
There'll be a 'cat flap' noise - now Dad'll miss the match.
Greetings meowed across the room, our little man's presence is felt.
He'll jump on a lap to ask for fuss - which heart this time, will melt.

Could cupboard love *be* what it's all about? -
Food's surely on his mind.
But eating done - he'll want more fuss and tricks up his coat,
he'll find.
He'll climb up high to purr in an ear, his pleasure is hard to miss.
Once he has your attention - with his nose, he'll give you a kiss.

He has a girlfriend who lives next door -
she's pretty and ginger and shy.
They play hide and seek in the bushes.
When she's caught, she jumps so high.
They chase around the garden and seem to have such fun.
Shimmying up and down trees, in and out of the fence, they run.

When everyone has gone for the day, he'll climb upon the chair.
He'll sleep away the hours until - on returning,
you'll find him still there.
He'll stretch his length and roll on his back -
'Tickle me' he'll seem to say.
Then off he'll rush to the kitchen to be fed - without delay.

A little man has come to stay. We're glad he's chosen us.
He's brought such pleasure into our lives - with his character
and his fuss.
He seems quite settled and wants to stay.
We want him to stay with us too,
With his fun-loving antics to keep us amused,
we love him so much -
wouldn't you?

L Northam

Woodstock

Nobody else would have him, sorry little mite,
Some children found him cold and scared, shivering with fright.
They took him round from door to door, 'Would you like a cat?'
But people laughed and said 'No thanks! Not an ugly thing like that!
It's out of all proportion, big feet and head so small.
Are you sure it's not part kangaroo, not a cat at all?'
He really was an oddity. Funny little thing.
Big feet, big ears, pixie face, tail like a piece of string!
Pathetic little bundle, body bony thin.
His huge sad eyes begged 'Let me stay. Won't someone take me in?'
'Please, Mum,' my sons were pleading,
Just then our ginger Tom came running, curious to see
What on earth was going on.
He ran up to the kitten, who bravely stood his ground,
We all watched with bated breath, afraid to make a sound.
Then Tiggy washed the kitten, as if to make it clear
He mustn't be so scruffy if he wanted to live here!
Since then they've been inseparable, together night and day,
The housework gets neglected as I watch them at their play.
And how our stray has blossomed! He's such a clever cat.
He opens cupboard doors, he begs, now just imagine that!
He's sort of grown together now. His funny look has gone.
In fact he's very handsome now, our *duckling* is a swan!

Edna Ridge

The Discovery

It was when we decided to move the shed
We found her nestling there
In a cosy little well-kept nest
Of grass and leaves, and fur
So, being extremely careful
A shelter we did build
Around the cosy little nest
From harm and cold to shield.

She'd take her daily scuttle
Around the garden's edge
Sniffing around the flowers
And underneath the hedge
Then, one bright sunny morning,
She proudly brought them out
Making sure no danger
Was lurking round about

Five little baby hedgehogs
Appeared out from the nest
Gently she nudged the first one out
Then went back in for the rest
When all were safely gathered
She led them carefully away
Well done little mother hedgehog
I hope you come back some day!

Dorothy Durrant

Fizzy Fred

We had an old dog named Fred.
He was always very busy.
He had such a zest for life
we used to call him Fizzy.
He was a funny little chap,
a crossed basset with a beagle.
We had a problem, when he ran,
he took off like an eagle.
He had little stubby legs,
and uncontrollable wanderlust.
When he decided he wanted to go,
we couldn't see him for dust.
It was very hard to tame him,
so of Fred there's now a lack.
Last time he had the urge to go,
he went and never came back.

Tracey Anne Toma

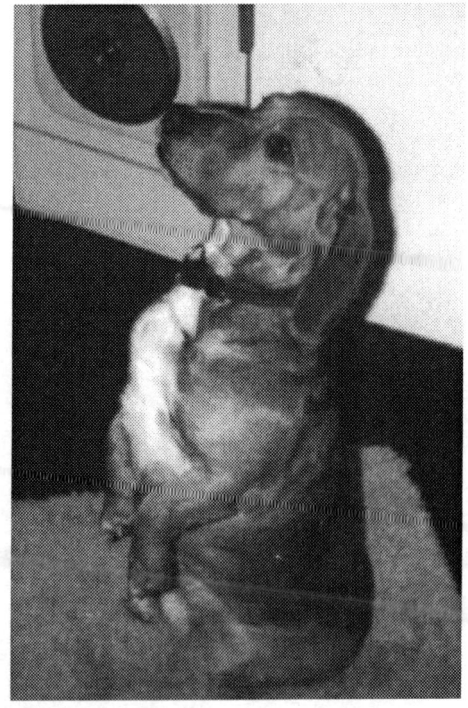

My Loving Vampire

She would wait for me
To cut my finger
And lick the drops of blood
With wild relish -
Eyes bright with golden fire -
Looking up and asking for more.

And often her long ivory white teeth
Made small black double bruises
In the flesh of my side,
And her sharp claws
Slashed my skin
With scars and punctures -
And all this was done for love.

She could have had my blood,
And when she needed my life force,
Although it was too late -
I held her soft old body
Through the night and gave her
My failing courage.

So when other people,
Mortals all, saw me carry
A sick little dog in a towel
To the vet -
They missed our symbiotic mingling
And could not understand
That part of me
Would be hers forever.

Mary Jane Hanscomb

A Shepherd Without Sheep

Now, our dog's a sheepdog
At least - he is by right.
The trouble is
Our garden's big -
But, not a sheep in sight!

It doesn't bother him,
Rounding up is what he does -
Next door's cats
The kids at play
Or flying things that buzz.

He's not all that successful,
Although he tries and tries
They won't comply
These things that fly -
Like bees and butterflies.

He makes a lot of noise
You should hear him when it's sunny
He barks and shouts
And runs about
It all looks rather funny.

The birds come down for worms
He charges like a pup
He's no idea
So they've no fear
They just fly off and up.

At last he stops to rest
And in his dreaming sleep
Tired out by play
It's the only way
He gets to round up real sheep.

Gill Morgan

Budgerigar

Leaf-green budgie, glowing bright,
Locked into your cage at night,
Free to roam the room by day,
On the highest shelf you stay,
Pensive, quiet - I know not why.
Suddenly alert, you fly
Like one in some unearthly dread,
Finally landing on my head.
Bird, you should be more suspicious,
When your name means 'most delicious'!
Soon, you realise your mistake,
Shuffle, shrug, again you take
Off, with strange and plaintive calls,
Grabbing curtains, windows, walls,
Mad and desparrot in your search
For the truly ideal perch.
Your house-hunting ventures fail;
Having tried the curtain rail,
You launch once more, and flap yourself
To your trusty wooden shelf.

Elizabeth Bullen

Ee, Four Dogs All T'Same

We had two Yorkshire terriers many years ago
One we named Tiny, the other one was Joe
We always took them with us when on holiday
There were two more Yorkies as with my aunt we went to stay
One was called Della, the other one was Scamp
A good name for him, and he stopped at every lamp
The four dogs we would take, it was such a game
Folks walking by said, 'Ee four dogs all t'same'
Della didn't belong, she lived in a pub.
But she had been naughty and began to grow a 'tub'
Scamp was the father, wouldn't you just guess
It was all his fault she was in this mess
Scamp, he was the boss, there was never any doubt
He'd let my Dad indoors, but he wouldn't let him out
His teeth dug in Dad's trousers, as he tightened his grip
We waited for the moment for the trousers to rip.
The look on our Joe's face didn't know what to make of that
Tiny wasn't bothered as she lay upon the mat
Then in Aunt Edie came, dog biscuits on a plate
Thank heaven for these as the dogs ate and ate
They soon ate the lot and while looking round for more
Dad took his chance, and slipped through the door
It happened all the time and we couldn't make a fuss
Nothing to laugh at, each time we missed a bus.

Joan Jeffries

Long Ago

Amber eyes, half closed but glowing,
Gaze unfathomed, and yet all knowing,
The subtle charm of a slender paw,
Outstretched, abandoned, on rug or floor,
Oh! What do you see, that inscrutable gaze,
A world of darkness, shade or haze,

You dream of chasing the morning sun,
As it moves around, your greatest fun,
To leap and dance at a wandering leaf,
A bee or butterfly, and fall in a heap,
To gaze once more at a shadowy figure,
You crouched, you stalked, then leapt with vigour,

Or were you dreaming of long summer days,
With nothing to do but your kittenish ways,
Your whiskers a-twitch, your pink nose a-quiver,
Along that bright coat, a sensuous shiver,
I think you dream of years far long gone,
In Egypt's fair land, with the Kings you were one,

Everyone bowed at your sepulchred shrine,
But now Mr Pussy, you're surely just mine,
I offer no more than a warm basket bed,
Food in your dish, and a garden to tread,
But happy you seem in spite of your schemes,
So eyes wide with wonder, go on with your dreams.

Grace Wade

The Crazy Man

They said, 'He's crazy'
He lived alone
In a hut in the woods
All on his own.
They said, 'He's mad';
And they never went near
And they taught their children
To hate and fear.
But this crazy man
In his little wood
Saw the primrose grow
And the blossom bud
And he heard the birdsong
Fill the air
And he saw the rabbit
Stand and stare
And the leaves unfold
On a springtime morn
And the nests of tiny birds new-born
He never harmed
A single thing
He tended the robin's
Broken wing
His friends were the badger
The squirrel, the dove
And he gave them his help
And his time and his love
But with trampling feet
The strangers came
With shotguns ready
To kill and maim
And the little wood rang
And shook with the sound
Of helpless creatures
Gunned to the ground.
He saw the slaughter
And felt the blows

And he ran from his hut
And he raged out; 'No'
They laughed at his sorrow
'He's only a clown
And if he's not quiet
We'll shoot him down.'
His wood became
A fearful place
And a river of tears
Ran down his face
And when they had gone
He wandered again
And saw the destruction
And bore the pain
He picked up a bird
Broken and dead
'What crazy fools
What madmen,' he said.

Sybil Sibthorpe

Ahmed - My Siamese Friend

From indifference
And rejection;
From unkind word,
And sad reflection,
I turn to him.
His soft brown fur;
His sapphire look;
His gentle purr
I much prefer
To human introspection.
He can relax
In the warm rays,
Ne'er tense nor tax
His halcyon days.
His personage calm
A quiet balm.
His faithful presence
Is the essence
Of nature's true perfection.

Mary Johnson-Riley

Tiddley

Tiddley is a pussy cat,
With black and ginger on her back,
Underneath she is all white,
And hates all men that come in sight.
Tiddley eats a lot of fish,
Then sits and purrs, and how I wish
That she would, a bit more friendly be
When people come and visit me.
She doesn't like strangers, not at all,
She makes then back against the wall,
Hissing and spitting and making a fuss,
She thinks she is protecting us.
She rubs her back against my feet
When it's time for her tinned meat.
We live in a flat, the cat is quite clean,
With dirtbox and cushion that's fit for a queen.
If she gets fleas I give her a bath,
She doesn't scratch, it's quite a laugh.
I fill the sink with water warm,
Then to her head the fleas all swarm.
And when she's wet and feeling sad
I rub her dry to make her glad.
She sits by the window to get some air,
No prettier cat I do declare.

June Barber

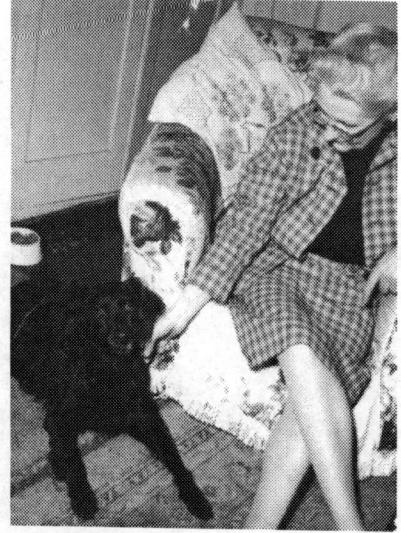

The Hedgehog

Trundling round the garden,
Hunting worms and beetles,
There's little that he fears
Armoured with his needles.

The dogs go yelping round him
Their muzzles pricked and sore.
He rolls a little tighter,
Thinks they are a bore.

Sniffing by the back door,
The cat's food's ready there.
Poor Tiddles spits and grumbles
He'll never get a share.

Be cautious in the autumn,
Sort the bonfire with great care.
Don't light it in a hurry,
Mr Prickles may sleep there.

Dorothy Morley

Trick Of The Light

Staring at the stormy lake,
bedazzled by an angel fish
fluorescing with a rainbow's range of hues,

I took the plunge to search that pool
and tried to catch the dancing shape,
but found my hands were struggling with an eel.

Despondent, soon I let it go,
still twisting like a corkscrew's ghost,
set up to crash in other murky thoughts.

The lake was licked by lightning bolts.
I swam, still keen to search the sheen
for treasures to admire in flickering waves.

Peter Comaish

The Deserted Cat

Far in the glen an old cat lies
Sheltered as best she may
Out of view the home she once knew
The family have gone away.
Without a care for their one-time pet
A daily friend from morn to night
Who took their food and felt secure
And in return gave much delight.

The family moved to another town
The cat was out, they did not wait
Leaving her to an empty house
Not knowing what would be her fate
She waited patiently outside
Hunger gnawing incessantly
Believing deeply in those she loved
That she would see them presently.

Alas the days remained the same
With no-one there to tend her needs
A titbit here and there she scrounged
Or caught a mouse among the weeds
Her heart was longing for those she loved
And she was cold that wintry day
When a new family came to the house
Saw the cat and chased her away.

She wandered through the barren fields
And ended in the sheltered glen
Glad to seek the lone sanctuary
Far away from the haunts of men,
Turning wild she hunts each day
Her victims eaten to the last
Cold and aching at night she dreams
Of the comforts of the past.

Thelma Paolozzi

Rescued

It was all my sister's fault
to take me where I really thought
the rescued animals left to roam
should all be safe with me at home.

And there we saw our 'Huxley pig'
whose mum and dad were small not big
a home was needed, so to us he was sold
a pot-bellied pig - only four weeks old!

The 14th Feb, a special day
for that's when Huxley came to stay
my Valentine's present from my husband was he
little did we know what a pickle he'd be

We had to move when Huxley was four
he just couldn't get inside the door
now he has a stable of his own
a plot of land where he can roam

He'll wander up to the house at seven
for his food, then he's in heaven
back midday and again at four
if he could, I know he'd eat more.

For the love he gives us, I could not measure
he really is a little treasure
everyone who's met him thinks the same
so don't forget 'Huxley' is his name.

Elaine Gofton

Friends

Faithful friends I have but two
One is old, one quite new
I love them both
And they love me

They are always by my side
Looking at me with eyes so kind
If I am down they brighten my day
At night by my side they will lay

We go out together us three
A walk in the park the ducks to see
Over the field and down the lane
Always together in sunshine and rain

My two faithful friends who are they
If they could talk I know what they'd say
Thank you for looking after us we love you
My doggy friends I love you too

P Ford

Sheba

She was a homeless dog
Wondering the street
No-one to talk to
No-one to meet

She wasn't wanted as a pet
But that all changed when we met
We stared at her, she stared at us
Her tail was wagging, she enjoyed the fuss

We paid the kennel money
And took her away
We bought her a toy
And watched her play

We've had a wonderful past
With our dog
She's better than a mouse
A rabbit or a mog!

Sheba's getting older now
She's sleeping most of the time
I hope she's remembering the days with us
When she was in her prime!

We love you Sheba!

Nicola Gedge (17)

Big Ben

Ben was power, a giant with pace,
'Strike Early' his apt track racing name,
Bred for speed, and trained to chase
For fame, in man's toughest betting game.

He'd come to us from a living hell,
Rescued, just in time, by the RSPCA,
Abused, starved, his body but a skeletal shell,
A price for failure much too harsh to pay.

Behind that hurt somewhat distant stare,
Lay a trauma of beatings, neglect, and pain,
And yet, slowly, Ben responded to care,
Learned to relax, and to trust people again.

He gave us years of real genuine pleasure,
Did Big Ben, our huge greyhound friend,
For hiding beneath that striking exterior,
Lay warm affection, and loyalty to the end.

His demise, when it came, caught us unawares,
Latent kidney disease had progressed apace,
Leaving Ben, acclaimed chaser of mechanical hares,
Finally outrun, in his last important race.

For dear Ben, death donned a painless disguise,
An injection brought his distress to an end,
And as life ebbed from those trusting eyes,
We cried - we'd lost a selfless family friend.

Andrew Farmer

Squirrel In The Garden

He wasn't mine, just kindly lent
God's jackanapes, but when he went
Spring went with him.

An empty stage, inviting lawn,
The gymnast leaps, keen to perform
His circus act.

Advance, retreat, tiptoe and hide,
Chatter and twirl, gallop and glide,
Teasing the cat.

A soundless flute, filigree fingers,
Hearing the note, springtime lingers
To catch his round.

Arrogant tail, cocking a snook,
A curving plume, a jester's look,
Sharp as a sword.

Quite warm, but still, at noon he lay,
Still warm, quite dead, his motley grey
Soft on the earth.

He wasn't mine, but when he played,
Spring was At Home, and while he stayed,
I felt . . . honoured.

Cherry Chapman

Instinct: Death At Dusk

Sleek, silent stealth, steel tipped
Talons tearing flesh.
Feathers fly, a cry, no more.
No mourning.
Offspring savour bloodied feast.
Peace for parents, a while at least.
Young bellies soon demand,
Instinct commands.
Food to grow, strength and skill,
Nature's masters of the kill.

Caroline de Carle

Kitty

Skinny as a rake is she, has been all her life
She's not anorexic, does not have any strife
Plays just like a baby even in old age
Can't read a book when she's about, (parks her bum on every page)
Chases mice, but just for fun, runs after the duck
Gets really, really huffy when paws get in the muck . . .
Hogs a lap in winter, in summer she's aloof
A lesson if you're in PR, for she's the living proof,
Treats the dog with great disdain, uses him with glee
Shares his dinner, hogs her own and loves a slurp of tea,
Any garden that gets dug, she's there quick as a flash
Neighbour blames her every time when she comes out in rash . . .
But when it comes to parting as on holiday we go
She will ignore us on return, keeps us at beck and tow,
If hubby and I parted, it really would be sad,
Decision time for her to make, to live with Mam or Dad . . .!

Margarette L Damsell

Pals

Steadfast and loyal, devoted and true,
they share in my joy and my sorrow.
Whatever befalls, they're there by my side,
not caring what may come tomorrow.

We tramp over hills, and walk through the woods,
no trio as happy as we.
All that they ask is to share in my love,
and spend all their time out with me.

They're not pedigrees, their ancestry's unknown,
a couple of mongrels they are.
But the love that they give, could not be surpassed,
by a winner of Crufts from afar.

My staunchest of pals are here by my side,
my every desire to fulfil.
If the whole world rejected me now,
They'd both love and comfort me still.

Give your love freely, and do not abuse,
your best friend so faithful and good.
Look after him well, he'll repay you tenfold,
and love you as all good dogs should.

Fred Wyer

Chameleon

Cast in moonlight I'm silver,
in the haze I'm a blur,
with the ice stones I'm crystal,
of me no-one's aware.

I am gold in the sun,
turn to green by the trees,
I go blue with the sky,
seems like nobody sees.

I stay clear in the rain,
changing white for the snow,
seen as black with the night,
I'm like no-one, I know.

I possess all the colours,
yet I can't choose the mode,
just a camouflaged bomb
that still waits to explode . . .

Andrew Clough

It's A Dog's Life

I'm waiting here so patiently,
Please take me for a walk,
I look at you so pleadingly,
I wish that I could talk;
I'd love to go into the park,
So I could jump and run,
Perhaps you'd throw a ball for me,
Oh wouldn't that be fun!
What can I do to make you move,
Get up out of that chair,
The TV's on and all you seem
To do is sit and stare;
Perhaps if I start barking,
You'll look up and notice me,
With a little bit of luck,
You'll understand my urgent plea;
So turn off the control knob,
And be mindful of my need,
It really isn't asking much,
'Please go and get my lead'.

Dorothy Neil

Urban Vixen

A female fox so chic and sheen
In electric glow is often seen
And passers by food to feed they lay
An inexpensive price to pay
To see God's nature in the raw
For as an animal of the wild
She breaks nature's law
Very quietly you have to stand
        But never touch
Quietly she will approach the hand
Staring at you in trust with glowing eyes
So tame she looks but just a guise.
For she will take the offering and then be gone
Back to the wild where she was born
But of late nature's song has not been sung
For is she not deep in earth with young.

Colin P Jennings

Who's Laughing

You see my face behind the fence,
I see you laugh and smile.
Some say I should be running free,
But just ponder a little while.
I know not what it's like to run
Across a dry grassy plain.
Search for each drop of water,
Little food causing hunger's pain
Hunted by man and lions,
Causing me to fight and feel fear.
Here I have food, water, shelter
And safety to give me cheer.
I will ask you something,
You haven't got a clue,
Are you laughing at my face
Or is it me laughing at you?

Josie Minton

Ossie And Katie

Two tiny ducklings, only 4 days old
Mother, Esmeralda, was killed on the road
We called the black one Ossie
Because he was so bold
Katie, we named the other so
          fragile to behold
Guess what?! Both now are large and strong
But Ossie is the lady and
          Katie is the drake!
How did we get it wrong?
What an awkward mistake!

Ethel Bestford

The Stray's Paradise

It's a wonderful thing to have a home -
I never had one before:
All they could do was shout and moan,
And then they showed me the door.

But somehow or other I found a friend
Who left me food to eat,
Who came and stroked me now and then
And gave me milk and meat.

I knew I was in with a chance, so I ran
To greet my friend one day
And rubbed and purred and pranced and sang
Till my friend took me away.

And now I find I have a home
With sunny spots and flowers
And fishy treats and meaty bones,
And the strokes go on for hours.

Silky

Lovely Laura

I always loved her as she was,
Gentle, dignified, affection plus.
She wore a coat as soft as silk,
As white as the snow on a distant hill.
One day I took her to a show,
For this gentle creature it was no go,
She hated all the noise and chatter,
So I took her home, did it really matter,
Then I thought about a litter,
Six pups were born, she was never fitter,
Four girls, two boys without a sound,
This bitch had really done me proud,
Two for the ring without a doubt,
What fun was had first time out,
Years slipped past Laura was nine,
Everything in her world was fine,
Until one day she missed a step,
Then missed again, she needs a vet,
Laura was given tests galore,
But there would never be a cure,
She found it difficult to walk,
So I sat beside her and softly talked,
I knew the time had come to part,
So with much sadness in my heart,
We went again to see the vet,
The vet was gentle and oh so kind,
He gave us so much of his time
And late that afternoon in June
I did the hardest thing to do,
To my lovely Laura I said adieu.

Jean Kington

The Fly

Just outside our kitchen door is a lovely patch of sun,
I love to lie there, with its warmth upon my tum,
I wriggle and stretch to expose every spot,
And 'cause I'm a little dog there's really not a lot.

I sigh and settle to have a lovely snooze,
When all at once there's a tickle on my nose,
I opened one eye, just to have a look,
There's one of those things my mistress swats with a book.

I opened my mouth and with a quick snap,
That fly I was hoping to trap,
But, with a buzz he circled my head,
Then landed on my belly instead.

Now instead of resting in the sun,
A hunt for that darned fly has begun,
Up the windows, on the wall,
I could not catch that fly at all.

So with resignation, and a little dread,
I just sit and watch it instead,
Now it's landed on the mat,
I'm off to sit on my mistress's lap.

Billie Moore

Snowy

Snowy was a rabbit,
She was very big and white,
All day she ran around outside,
And came indoors at night.
Our brown and white Jack Russell
Slept nightly at her side,
And she missed her just like we did,
When our dear Snowy died.
Although she was so very old
I couldn't help but cry,
When Snowy had to leave us
For that warren in the sky.
I hope we'll meet again some day,
In that glorious realm above,
For it wouldn't seem like Heaven
Without the animals we love.

Ivy Neville

A Catty Conversation

A catty conversation, I overheard one day,
Now, here is some translation, of what I heard them say.
'Good morning, my dear Tinker, you do look glum just now.'
'Well, Tabby, I'm no whinger,' said Tinker, 'you'll allow,
But I've got human trouble and from that house I fled,
The children are my grumble and they fill me with bread.
My tail so often twisting, or pulling at my hair,
I could go on, things listing, what often does occur
And, when upon one turning, a little scratch I gave,
A blow I was soon earning, my mistress said '*Behave.*'
The children are just heartless and much too rough for me,
Now, I just long for kindness, a better home to see.'
'Next door, there is a soft one,' said Tabby, 'that's for sure,
You play your part today, son, when she comes to her door.
Look up, your front paws raising, with head upon one side,
You'll find it most amazing, no food will be denied.
So, Tinker, stop your fretting, if you will now persist,
Before long, she'll be petting, no purr can she resist.
You'll get good meals each day there and milk, all you could wish,
But, one thing you must not dare, don't come and eat my fish.'
The lady soon appearing, Tinker was very wise.
She found him most endearing, saw him on hind legs rise,
In making his petition, he seemed to her so sweet,
That a family addition just made her day complete.
Here is the happy ending, no more does Tinker roam,
His view of life amending, finding a happy home.
Man does have his dominion o'er animals, we know,
But it is God's instruction that we should kindness show.
Cruelty in this world should always be deplored,
The cruel one, the least is in the kingdom of the Lord.

Donald J Price

Cindy

Since you've been gone;
I've learnt to carry on;
Though the memories I still hold;
And my love for you untold.

You're face when you past;
No more pain for you at last.
You stared at the wall;
Wouldn't look at me at all.

And when the needle went in;
I couldn't say a thing.
I cried from ten till seven;
'Cause I knew you'd left for heaven.

Although it's been over a year;
I still miss you near.
I think of you all the time;
So to you, I dedicate this rhyme.

And when I'm feeling low;
I know just where to go.
To a field where we used to sit;
And then I'll sit and cry a bit.

But I know you're always near,
I can sense you in the air.
And I'll start to smile and say;
'Cindy, I'll see you again some day.'

Lisa Jane Bevan

Forever Gold

Brimstone butterfly
On a pale June evening
Pasted on the plaited roots
Of a forest grove
Under ancient beechen eaves
Lighting up the littered leaves
Countless as its days of
Brief eternity.

S A Fargher

One In A Lifetime

To the stranger he gives a warning
wags his tail to those he knows
but he really is a one man dog
and by his actions it shows.

When out walking on the street
he never needs a lead
he waits patiently by the shop doors
to other dogs and people he pays no heed.

In the house at night when we're alone
he does not bark or growl
at the slightest noise he pricks his ears
and then goes on the prowl.

He is protective after dark
and sleeps by my bedroom door
he never moves away from there
until he hears me cross the floor.

He was the smallest one of the litter
the weakest one in the run
in a lifetime you only get one like him
he has a quality second to none.

So now old friend I salute you
I would miss you if you were gone
may your life always be happy
and your time with me be long.

Frank Scott

My Best Friend

You give me unconditional love and devotion,
Never doubting my love you're always there,
With special senses, you know when all is not well,
You're always there comforting and soothing,
Never needing to be told when teatime comes around,
You're not fussy you know you'll get the best.

Outside you will go, not far will you stray,
Soon back you arrive, from who knows where.
Quietly almost silently you enter my room,
Head and tail held high with an air of regal grace,
Stepping over my feet, your touch as a whisper glancing by.

Carefully taking your time you wash and groom,
So fastidious, inspecting and checking your coat.
Satisfied you nestle down beside me,
Resting, contentedly sleeping until mealtime again,
Sleep peacefully, my devoted cat.
My Charlie.

Carolyn Foggin

A Special Companion

The first thing we saw through a caged door
was such a sight, a thin and shabby mite
lying all alone, not belonging to anyone
a seven-year-old collie cross breed, Shandy was your name
your bad attitude was caused by no-one loving you
and despite how we cared, you'd fight us all the way
I still remember those days, but how times have changed

You'll follow us around like a shadow, with a sparkle in your eyes
you're so full of life, sometimes competing in runs alongside
you'll wag your tail when happy
and your black coat is so silky and gleams with being clean and healthy
you hate to be left out and love being taken out
enjoy breaks away, but after coming back you'll sulk for days

Every morning to wake us up, you'll place a smelly sock in our face
then before eating your food, you'll sit and give me your paw to shake
when a stranger calls, you'll make such a noise
just letting them know, you're only protecting us from any harm
and you think life is so unfair, when you can't get your own way
and if my Dad forgets to give you a treat, you'll give him a sad pathetic glare
making him feel like he just doesn't care
and you love to swim in rivers and lakes but when it comes to bath time
you're always the same, being stubborn and trying to run away
when drying out, it looks like you've had crimpers in your fur

You can be sweet and gentle as can be
but on off days, you're not very well behaved, to be honest you're quite a pain
still so nervous and sometimes snappy too
despite your faults we couldn't part with you
that would be the easiest thing to do,
though you might not think so at times
you'll always be a special dog to us, who will always be loved so very much

V Salt

The Ballad Of The Cats

'Candy' we named our dear little tabby;
She'd been the victim of treatment shabby,
Though in a few weeks you scarce would guess
An abandoned waif once was this princess.

She had all the airs of a high-born puss,
Despite her privations, fastidious,
Eyes pools of amber, dainty of paw,
A cute little face in a halo of fur.

She reigned as a queen until one day we moved,
An event of which she quite disapproved;
We hunted her everywhere, agonised,
Despairing, in newspaper advertised.

Then Tigger turned up, right out of the blue,
Took over the place as only he knew;
No beauty was he; a gregarious chap,
Brought in all his friends through Candy's cat-flap.

Till one day the phone rang; said a friendly voice:
'I think I've found Candy!' - Did we rejoice!
She'd been living wild; now, with tigress-like ire,
The usurper she chased from her place by the fire.

Tigger sprang at his rival, bearing his claws,
Snatched a chunk of her fur with a snap of his jaws;
With frantic miaow Candy leapt on my knee,
Disdainfully snarled at such temerity.

The cat-flap crashed noisily: Tigger was gone,
Too proud to stay not to be number one;
When out for a walk I met him one day,
He rubbed close against me and went on his way.

Tigger was a roamer, Tigger came to call,
He would settle on his terms, or not at all.

Betty Everson

Simian Satire

Having some time to kill during a short stop-over,
And being a genuine and dedicated animal lover.
I resolved to ask directions and explore a German zoo.
I wandered around the park, feeling extremely impressed,
Because the care and housing of the animals was of the best.
The bears could lumber, the hippos wallow and the gazelles prance.
Then I saw it, standing aptly decorated - the pièce de resistance!(?)
Beside the ape enclosure had been built a climbing frame.
Many young visitors thought it a wonderful game,
To climb and swing and posture in their gaudy clothes -
Did they guess the structures real purpose, d'you suppose?
For the enlightened designer had erected it to amuse the apes!
And riveted they were, by the ridiculous humans' jolly japes.
Those dignified simian giants, whilst watching the colourful hordes,
At last had something entertaining to prevent their getting bored!

Linda Miller

To Cull Or Not To Cull

The twilight hour, enchanted glade
Shimmering wraiths and misting shade
A magic cottage, rose-embowered
With winding pathways, deeply flowered
Ox-eye and cowslip flourished there
And rabbits played with the mad March hare.
Peace and enchantment closed around
Sweet smelling blossom, silvery sound
Of stream that gurgled on and on
Round the feet of the great, black Groen,
King of dogs - he raised his head
Thinking it was his master's tread.
His warning bark had scarcely died
I saw his master by his side.
Love and devotion shot between
The two of them, both felt and seen
We talked, the air with sadness filled
He told me how his wife was killed,
His children too. And so, bereft,
Only despair and tears were left
His big, black, regal Groenendal
Nuzzled his hand, and moved his tail.
'He was the runt, and should be dead,
But he was my kiss of life,' he said.

Man made the standard of the breed,
But who created a human's need?
And who shall say that a pup shall die
If his eyes are round or his ears set high?
Breed carefully, breed beauty if you will
But do not needlessly set out to kill
Remember, the babe that you decide to cull
Might be the 'kiss of life' to some poor soul.

Penny Scales

Once An Alley Dog!

What is he writing about
    me
I find out by
    tail-epathy
Besides the *call*, a *nod*
    or winking
I know exactly what he's thinking
That poems all comprised
    of noughts!
I'm so-so with these
    two-way thoughts
I know he loves and
    cares for me
The life of riley
    my own tree
A member of the
    Kennel Club
But me sleep out?
    Give that the *rub*
As I say it goes
    both ways
I run and jump
    it's him that *plays!*
He's writing of
    the *doggy-world*
I'm black 'n' tan
    my rudder curled
No sheepdog greyhound,
    guard, as much
Crufts! - Ye gods
    cows fly, or such?

Liam McKinney

Animal Love . . .

Love animals? So be sentimental
About a dog, delightful furry thing,
Call him your 'pet', destroy his dignity,
Forget the wolf that lurks, renunciation
Of his native steppe . . . snarling delight
Of combat as a pack, no quarter given
To others or his kind . . . the tireless hunting,
Of this proud and furious carnivore.

The sleek and lovely horse which your hand
Has curry-combed, whose once wild tarpan spirit
Is quite tamed away . . . he'll take your carrot
With gentlest mouth, suffer your idle stroking
Of nose and mane . . . he will take your weight
Day-long in patience, will not even jerk
You into a ditch with his legs back-kicking,
And trumpet-neighing, fling away in joy!

Hypocrites that eat some animals:
Deer that have become domestic cows,
The pig that was the terror of the thicket
Whence man did flee! . . .
                         But I know you'd rather
Enjoy the easy flattery of these
Programmed like robots to make you feel good
And even sentimental, on these terms . . .

Austin Cooper

Wanted!

Have you seen this dog?
This handsome posing model,
Locally knows as 'the bad bedroom raider'
Aka Nipper our Jack Russell.

Note his painted face-mask of tan,
Don't be fooled by his looks!
He's dangerous, and shouldn't be trusted -
He may well run off with your sock!

Keep your pockets zipped-up,
Shut all bedroom doors,
He'll root through your possessions -
The bandit on four paws!

Laura England

Pedro

His fur was burnished like the noon-day sun,
As if it had absorbed its gilded rays,
Which fell in rich profusion, one by one,
To make a coat with golden lights ablaze.

His eyes like amber beads with flecks of gold
Could flash like lightning on a stormy night,
Or simulate deep sadness as they rolled
To cast a spell on everyone in sight.

His splendid ears like pendant earrings fell,
And, as he walked, they swayed from side to side,
Like russet leaves a-flutter in the dell
When gentle zephyrs would not be denied.

This wicked rascal thought it was no sin
To bite the towels blowing in the breeze,
Then clench his razor teeth and dig them in,
Swinging aloft with acrobatic ease.

When he was big enough to reach the shelf
Where biscuits were contained in boxes tall,
He thought it would be fun to help himself
By pulling with his paw to tip them all.

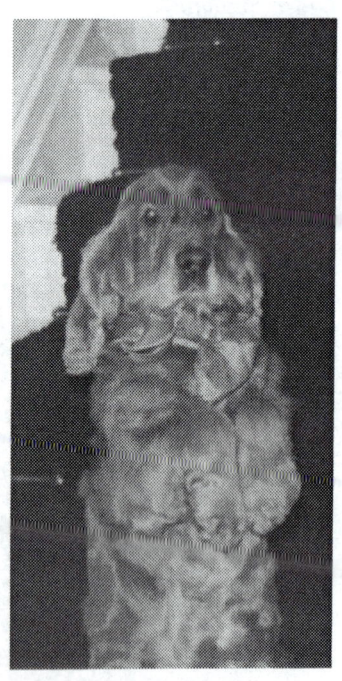

Like mighty Hector at the walls of Troy,
With muscles flexed he guarded his domain.
It was his sacred duty and his joy
To keep a watch and there he would remain.

At last time dimmed the sparkle in his eyes,
And silvered whiskers shone amid the gold.
He could not run so fast nor jump so high;
We knew our treasured friend was growing old.

The great god Pan came sadly down to earth
And watched the agéd spaniel as he slept.
He'd loved this creature even since his birth,
But now this last appointment must be kept.

Celia G Thomas

My Best Friend

His staring, appealing, hazel-brown eyes
   follow my movements when I arise.
      Patiently waiting till I speak his name
         then up on all fours to play his first game.

He picks up his ball and brings it to me,
   his tail wagging efforts expend energy.
      I play hide and seek with the ball, just to tease;
         he sits on his haunches as if to say please.

His doleful expression tugs at my heart;
   I show him the ball and we make a fresh start.
      With a lead on his collar we go for a walk
         the air's filled with noises, he barks and I talk.

I tell him about the times I once knew,
   tales of misfortune that made me feel blue.
      He senses the difference in my tone of voice
         then tugs on the lead and gives me no choice.

His movement has disturbed my sad reverie
   bringing my thoughts back to reality.
      Time to return for breakfast and then
         do a few chores and go walkies again.

We live for the moment in close harmony.
   My dear little dog is the whole world to me.
      So closely bonded, my very best friend
         forever together, until journey's end.

Stan Taylor

The Best Of Friends

I have a friend who's brown and white, a proper little beauty,
When I go out, he goes too, we go to do our duty.
Along the path and down the lane and then on to the grass,
And there we have a sniff about and watch as people pass.
Dad then comes out and calls us in, I wish that we could stay,
But we're good boys, that's what he says, so him we do obey.
Back up the lane, along the path, the two of us, kind of slouch,
Run through the house, to the front room and jump up on the couch.
I've got to go out, he says to us, I'll be back again, about ten,
And when I do, if you've been good, I'll let you out again.
When he has gone, we have a ball, we really do have fun,
Up the stairs and down again, all through the house we run.
I think you may have guessed by now, that we are rather jolly,
But did you guess, that I'm a boxer and my friend's a spaniel-collie.
My name is Zak and I am white, Patch is white and brown,
We often sit at Dad's window, when he is down the town.
Yes I am Zak and he is Patch, sadly, here my story ends.
But one more thing, I'd like to say, we are *The Best of Friends*.

Robert Kerr

Major

It's true you know!
That a dog is man's best friend,
The love and kindness,
That you give to them,
They will return to you.

I lost a friend,
So wonderful was he,
My days he filled with happiness,
Always there for me.

Major would sit so close,
His head upon my knee,
These moments were so precious,
Just having him near to me.

The memories such happy times,
The walks we took,
He looked so magnificent,
Walking at my side,
My heart would swell with pride.

The happiness he gave to me,
I will cherish my life through,
A faithful and a loving friend,
Until the very end.

I'll always keep a place,
Deep in my heart,
Especially for you,
For darling this I know is true,
I'll never find another you.

Terri Brant

I Heard A Nightingale

I heard a nightingale
From my room in this place.
It sang so sweet,
I returned to God's grace.

I sat in despair,
In this hall for the old.
But I heard a nightingale,
And was once more consoled.

They sit and they wait,
Their minds in the past.
But I heard a nightingale,
And despond from me cast.

I heard a nightingale,
From my room in this place.
It was so brave,
Where hope has no trace.

Frederick Manning

Bone Of Contention

I am called Skippy and I live up to my name,
I couldn't be described as boring or plain.
And so, when my owner was told of a show,
She thought it an excellent idea for to go.

She hoped for at least the best in my class
And so she was given a competitors' pass.
I skipped round the ring with a delicate air,
Kept my eyes on my mistress, and oh they did stare.

I could see she was proud, her face lit with joy,
She bent down and told me, 'You are a good boy.'
But then, when they asked us to walk round once more,
I thought, 'Oh no! This is becoming a bore.'

So all round the show ring we walked once again,
I followed behind a dog with no brain.
When we stopped in a line, I sat down in relief,
When, 'Bless me', this woman came to look at my teeth.

'I'm not having that,' thought I. 'What a cheek,
I'm going to show her, my teeth are not weak.'
But, I'm afraid, that was the end of our chances,
Of gaining a prize or admiring glances.

I gave her a nip on the hand to warn, 'Please beware',
She said it was because someone had cut off my hair.
I turned my back, you'd have thought she'd have known,
The only thing wrong was, I needed a bone.

M C Taylor

Amber Forever

My faithful dog Amber has charm and grace
Her soft brown eyes are set in a pretty face
With a coat like silk, it has a beautiful shine
I am proud to say that this dog is mine.

Walking for miles across fields and roads together
Side by side we journey on, in all kinds of weather
Sometimes I trail behind and Amber becomes the leader
My companion is at my side whenever I need her.

When our long walks are over, I am often flagging
With energy to spare Amber licks me, her tail is still wagging
I bend to stroke her soft head, knowing everything is all right
Ever faithful my little friend, snuggles up to me tight.

Her temperament is perfect, even strangers she will lick
Always playing seek and fetch, bringing back a stick
Everyone knows Amber, she brings pleasure to anyone who is near
Although she is a German shepherd dog, they have nothing to fear.

My affection for her is plain to see and this I am sure she knows
Because she responds to my emotions, by her actions her love for me shows
Having Amber for my constant companion forever grateful I will be
Following me just like my shadow, this bundle of mischief belongs to me.

Brenda Casburn Colvin

My Dog Bengy

My dog Bengy is not just a pet to me
he's like my very best friend you see

He's always there when I've had a bad day
and he'll never leave me if I ask him to stay

He greets me with pleasure each time we meet
and he'll love me forever if I give him a treat

I can't stay mad at him for very long
together is the way we'll always belong

I knew we'd be mates from the day he came here to live
and he'll always get all the love and trust I can give

We'll take care of each other and enjoy each day as it comes
and we'll always remain the very best of chums

Susan Rowe

Lion

King of the beasts noble lion, with your long mane hanging free,
Leo the sign I was born in, so it unites you and me.
Gentle your features when resting, tenderly watching your young,
Their mother contented beside them, for one more day now is done.

King lion was out hunting early, finding food for family,
Mother had cubs in the river, making them clean as could be.
Then they had lessons in stalking, when older must seek their own prey,
Learning to do this with father, for young ones there's no better way.

As they move through the green forest, so many creatures they meet,
Leopards, cheetahs and monkeys, making their world so complete.
Striped tiger will growl in false anger, King Leo with paw gives a swipe,
Both then go in different directions, neither in mood for a fight.

Relaxed and so casual they all look, as they amble through the rough ground
But if attacked can defend selves, as many others have found.
Paddling in the cool river, cubs play at catching some fish,
Mother still carefully watching, life always this peaceful, her wish.

Suddenly animal attacks cubs, frightening them with his roar,
King Leo at once is beside them, meaning to pay off this score.
Slashing and growling so fiercely, ripping at flesh to draw blood,
Then the attacker gets hurt so, rushes away into wood.

Mother and cubs go to help King, licking his wounds them to heal,
Then while King Leo is resting, mother produces a meal.
Cubs look wide-eyed at their parents, for a big lesson have learned,
Life is not all golden sunshine, brutality too has its turn.

Barbara Goode

Arabian Magic

The Arabic wind is all he needs
No running water, plants or trees
His heart is strong, and mind so pure
For this addiction there is no cure
As he trots through the heat
His body moving to the strongest beat
His heart is never lost
In conditions of the hardest test
For you he will always do his best
Respect and love are your only tasks
To honour his courage is all he asks!

E Blenkinsop

Why Do We Race Pigeons

See that tiny speck John, high up in the sky
Quickly getting nearer, trying hard to fly
steadfast and with purpose, one thing on its mind
to get back to its mate and nest in a minimum of time.

Look! It's one of ours John heading for the loft
Quickly get a thimble and put it in the clock
Gosh, we've got a good one there. Didn't it fly fast?
With the velocity that it's done we'll surely not be last

Come back and sit on your stool John and let your heart beat steady
all this fuss about racing and I nearly wasn't ready.
I'll make a cup of coffee and we'll wait for another
after all we also sent the winning pigeon's mother.

So ends the day of racing and looking back you remember
All the work that was needed when they were so much younger
the mating of the cock and hen, care taken with the breeding,
mixing of the corn and seed to make the proper feeding.

Look John, the 'old lady' has laid two more eggs for us
See how her cock bird is making so much fuss
bringing bits of straw and twigs to strengthen up the nest
So much work to do he'll hardly ever rest.

Twenty or so days later she's hatched out her two chicks
Greedy tiny squeakers - featherless bodies on two sticks.
Ugly little creatures, yelling for their food
constantly need sitting if we're to get a decent brood.

Hatched, then weaned, then flying, dropping from a height.
They don't know what to do yet but must be in by night
Put them in a basket and take them training tosses
be prepared for heartache when you find you've had some losses

See that tiny speck John, high up in the sky.
Get that excited feeling and then we both know why
All the work we've done, John has now come to its prime.
Work out the velocity - she's flown a record time.

Anne Dunnill

The Robin

It's with a sense of joy we see
The robin, wherever he goes:
On summer's lustrous leaf-green lea,
Or on winter's white-clad meadows.
The symbol of such happy days,
The red breast is a joy to see;
Thoughts of yuletide and festive ways,
Of nature and an empathy.
Yet 'neath that bright red breast so proud,
Lie bitter pride and jealousy;
The robin fights for territory,
By instinct he's a peaceless bird;
His presence only marks how near
Is the peaceless time we have each year.

Chris Moores

Max

It is now almost six years,
Since I sat you on my lap,
A little tiny bundle,
Trembling and black.

You looked at me with big brown eyes,
A tiny tongue gave a lick,
You curled into a ball of fluff,
Trembling and black.

We had a list of names,
Not knowing what to pick,
We read them all out to you,
At 'Max' you gave a lick.

So, Max you became, and Max you stayed
And together we grew friends
We all became a family
And with the children you played

You do not now sit upon my lap
Although you seldom do try
At two feet high and just as wide
A beautiful dog, not trembling, but black.

Margaret McQuilton-Morgan

Abandoned

I remember a home - laughter and fun
and warmth and walks and love
and a master who'd say 'Come on girl'
But it's all gone
I sit in my kennels, and memories make me cry.
He'll come back - he loves me.

I sit in my lonely kennel and sadness is all around
I can't remember faces or fun,
only a voice that used to say 'Come on girl'
But it's all gone.
I hope he'll come back, I thought he loved me.

I lie in this desolate kennel.
No-one comes, no-one laughs,
no-one calls 'Come on girl'
I lie here and cry, I just want to die.
I try to remember the voices, the home,
but it's all gone.
He won't come back, he never loved me at all.

Enid Hockenhall

Animal Magic

Baa baa black sheep hasn't any wool
It's sheep shearing day
And the sheep shearer's bag is full
The three blind mice aren't blind now you see
They had an 'op' on the National Health
And their sight's as good as can be
Nellie the elephant packed her trunk but not 2 go 2 the circus
Booked a holiday on a jumbo jet
She's in Australia watching the surfers
The red, red robin is still bob bobbin' along
Got an audition for 'Birds of a Feather'
And twice nightly sings a song
Ride-a-cock-horse to Banbury Cross
Not these days, he loves sunshine
And is holidaying in Andalucia of course
Skippy the bush kangaroo knows what he's going to do
He'll hop on a plane come to England in the rain
And visit relatives in London Zoo
Tony the tiger thought, to join the Army was right
But he didn't like taking orders
And was stripped of all his stripes
Micky and Minnie decided, that they'd like to retire
And to Blackpool they came, it's such a shame
'Cos! Their contracts haven't yet expired
Porky the pig thought himself for the chop, but apparently
He was mistaken
MGM had a contract with the Danes
For him to 'model' for Danish bacon
So it's goodbye from all in our menagerie
And hope we'll see them tomorrow on our TV's
Which is a distinct possibility

Sandra Witt

A Horse To Ride

Many love singing and dancing too,
High jinks and drinking, theatres and films,
Aircraft and travel, trains and TV,
Tractors and combines, working machines,
But give me a horse, a horse to ride,
With a silken mane and a swinging tail,
A straight, free mover with a loose stride,
Plenty of front and a head held high,
Flat flinty bone and a good blue hoof,
Deep at the throat with a bold clear eye,
Chestnut or grey, black-brown or bay.

A horse, a horse to ride, or a pony to drive,
Along, hedge bound lanes bordered with flowers,
Butterflies, bees and birds in profusion,
No speeding cars, lorries or coaches,
No crashes, nor curses with bumps and confusion.
A horse, a horse to ride in sunshine or showers
Across the fields to shepherd the sheep or call up the cows,
Out along droves where the curlews cry,
Over the moors at a canter
To carry good news or to visit a friend
To ride out together with laughter and banter.

Home to a bedded-up stable,
Hay and oats or a linseed mash,
Take care of your horse as best you are able,
Before your own needs, or so I was taught.

Oh give me a horse, a horse to ride,
Or a horse to drive,
To work in the plough and the harrow,
        the rake and the binder,
For seed time, hay time and harvest,
To restore the wealth of the land you gave us.
To slow down the world and lessen the stress
Thank you great God for your wonderful gift of the horse.

Elizabeth Mills

The Highlander

(Passed suddenly from this life 23.6.97 -
a dear friend and loyal companion)

I am a black
Scottish terrier
Stout hearted
Not shy
No 'wee shrinken violet'
I'm a wise
Fearless - old guy

My flowing beard
Matches whiskers
Of dense raven lock
And mine is
The prize name of
'Sandy' - or
Och aye the noo
Jock!

Irene Gunnion

A Dog's Life

Both my master and
    mistress,
Go out to work, each
    day,
They leave me chained
    up,
Unable to run and
    play.

They confine me to
    the garden,
At 8am each
    day,
'Be good, don't make
    a noise,'
Are all the words
    they say.

They do not understand,
that a big dog, like
    me,
Needs to run, in the
    long grass,
And use the occasional
    tree.

I am man's best friend,
And yet, I live like
    this,
Freedom and exercise,
Are the very things
    I miss.

The boredom, drives me
    crazy,
The same thing, every day
Don't do this to your
    dog,
Take him out, to run
    and play.

Show him kindness, and
    affection.
Give a little praise,
He will remain, forever,
A sincere and faithful
    friend.

Brian Morris

Winston

Brown eyes, innocent, staring;
A cold, wet nose in my hand.
Your life with me you'll be sharing
-Tell me - I'll try to understand.

Always a happy greeting,
Leaping, tail wagging, 'Play with me',
Irrespective of who you're meeting,
No evil do you ever see.

Faithful, loyal and constant love,
Such candour is in man so rare -
A gift bestowed by Him above
Who puts these creatures in our care.

My coat and boots are ready,
Your lead you fetch with glee,
Keen gaze, expectant, steady,
Outside we're wild and free.

Our daily walks give pleasure,
The woodland paths we roam.
Fond memories we treasure
Of countryside and home.

Now you're in your fourteenth year,
Together we have trod life's ways.
Winston, you are forever dear,
Just love has filled your doggy days.

Mary Farrell

Our Pup Heidi

I have a pup and Heidi is her name
chewing and playing is her favourite game
I plant pretty flowers, to make things look nice
along comes our pup and makes all kinds of strife

Back outside I go and re-plant my plants
that I love so, and guess who comes along
yes you know.

Heidi my faithful friend, who has a love
that has no end, but little does she know
that she can drive me round the bend.

She can be worse than my kids when
there at their best.
But when I've had enough, she knows
when to rest.
Her coat is so smooth, and black as soot
Her red collar gives her the 'just so' look
Heidi you're just a pup, but one day you'll
grow up.
A true and faithful friend you'll be, and
no-one will love you as much as me.

T J M Walker

My Best Friend

Her velvet-like coat of silky black fur
When happy and contented she'd sit and just purr
Her eyes of saffron yellow shone in the dark
Her ears would prick up if she heard a dog bark

At the bowl of milk her pink tongue would be lapping
Her long bushy tail never still but constantly flapping
Her black rubber nose always moist to the touch
The soft pads on her paws she loved tickled so much

Her black wiry whiskers turned white as she grew old
A creature of comfort, hated going out in the cold
She would run down the path when I arrived home
Would keep me company when I was alone

She seemed to understand every word I would say
She loved to be cuddled, she loved to play
She didn't roam far would appear in no time at all
Her oil painted portrait now adorns my lounge wall

One sad August day the time came for her to go
Now buried in the back garden that she loved so
She stuck by me right up till the very end
Not just a pet cat but my best friend

Linda Brown

Soliloquy To A Ridgeback

The Ridgeback is
   a noble beast,
Kind eyes, flop eared, and brow that's creased,
Deep chest, firm limbs
   and padded feet,
A tail that wags to masters greet.

He's headstrong yet
   a faithful hound.
A curious mind for all around.
To know a dog
   of such repute
So honest, wise, he doth us suit.

Rhodesia is
   the country whence
Came Ridgebacks from the grasslands dense
To guard, alone
   or hunt in packs
Wild cats, baboon, all fear he lacks.

This dog, how high
   his mind we rate.
To own one is a worthwhile fate.
How lithe his gait,
   he strides with speed.
My tribute to this special breed.

Nina J Jarman

Cobalt Blue

A tiny body firm and compact
In perfect proportion and intact
A personality far larger than life
Then illness struck suddenly threatening your life

Fluffed out feathers, looking sad
Ignoring your food, no mere fad
Eyes closed tightly, listless and ill
I stayed close beside your cage until
Your suffering eased

Lovable and humorous, our dear little friend
Cobalt blue budgerigar, brave to the end.

Rita Humphrey

A Visit From Harley

Daily he came,
Time the same.
Not for coffee or the *pain*,
But bacon sizzling in the pan.
Fringed at the window,
Paw on the door.
An old French kitchen, neat tiled floor.
He drooled at the table, waiting for more
Of that bacon sandwich, pure 'anglais,'
Plus toast and marmalade, 's'il vous plait.'
Harley's the name,
Of Davidson fame.

Tuesday we left, closed the door.
Does Harley miss us, or the bacon more?

Meg Pybus

Muffin

I'm a little dog called Muffin
It's short for something posh
They call me lots of other things
Especially when they're cross

I've got a nice home really
But it gets me down at times
There's this other dog called Megan
And she does everything just fine

Meg races round the lawn with me
And plays a game of ball
The trouble is she gets there first
'Cause she's very very tall

The other day the postman called
We hate him, me and Meg
One day we'll catch him if we can
And bite him on the leg

Why do I have to have a bath
All that soap and scrubbing
I'd rather stay just as I am
A scruffy dog called Muffin

Joyce Clifford

Grey Squirrel

So, you are back in my garden
Grey squirrel hiding from me;
I saw you from my window
Scamper up the apple tree.

Endearing little creature,
Bushy tail arched close and neat,
Sitting on your haunches,
Twirling food as you eat.

I know very well your intention
To take every nut contained there,
With never a thought for little birds
Coming home to a cupboard quite bare.

Which reminds me, I must be careful
Not to cool food on the shelf,
For you'll soon be through my window,
Quite happy to help yourself!

But in spite of all your mischief,
And knowing a thief you can be,
I'm really delighted to see you
On a branch of my apple tree.

Amelia Canning

That Cat

To see her sit and wash her face,
You'd never guess she's in disgrace,
But she just ate the master's fish.
Stole the lot from the dish.

Now as I threats and swear words whisper,
She cleans herself from tail to whisker.
Why did she have to choose today,
To act in this dishonest way?

The shops are closed I can't buy more
She now inspects a snowy paw!
In the larder, eggs cheese and ham
I'd best get out the omelette pan.

What he'll say I cannot think
She licks away with tongue of pink,
He's home he sniffs and looks surprised
While I start to apologise.

'Sorry there's no fish for tea,'
But look he's smiling happily
'I really get quite tired of plaice'
And plants a kiss upon my face.

He eats his tea with much delight,
'Why Sal how clean you look tonight'
He lifts her up upon his knee
And there she purrs contentedly.

Jean Roughton

It Must not Happen

Once there were whales, great creatures of the sea,
Patrolling their territory in the watery depths,
But their future was cut off by the globe's apathy,
Whilst heartlessly massacred, as the heedless world slept,
Magnificent mammals, hunted to death.

Once there were elephants, who no longer we see,
Mercilessly stalked for their white ivory,
And few were the voices in protest raised
Against their annihilation, to promote this vile trade,
Whilst the poacher exulted in the fortune he made.

Once there were tigers, untamed and proud,
Their roar in the jungle chilling and loud,
Beautiful felines, killed for their penis and skin,
While the world scarcely noticed the foul deeds happening.

Once there were butterflies bright in the air,
And the bumble bee buzzing around everywhere,
Many of these have had their day
Destroyed by the pesticides and chemical spray.

And the bird population has sadly declined
The corncrake and swallow are now hard to find,
And the skylark's sweet singing, no longer we hear
And how many others will soon disappear?

There is a real danger these things will come true,
It's already happening, what can we do?
Don't leave it to governments, it's down to me and you,
Imagine a world silent, without the birds melody,
Where wildlife is designated to past history,
Where the sprays and the poachers have won the day,
And the animals' habitats are taken away,
We must spring into action, before it's too late
Or the hands of the clock will have decided their fate.

Marjorie D Walshe

The Zoo

Today I'm going to the zoo,
To see the lions and tigers too.
What I like most about coming here,
Is the animals have nothing to fear.
Although they should all be free,
They are safer here than from man you see.
Because when they are in the wild and not the zoo,
Shoot them dead is what a hunter would do.
He will skin it and turn it into a coat for his wife,
How can he take an innocent creature's life?
The hunter has no feelings, he just doesn't care,
Would he kill and skin his children?
No he would not dare.
What have the lions and tigers ever done to him?
He deserves to be torn from limb to limb.

Gemma Reeman

Hoots Man

When the sun hides her face
   and the moon shows no light
hoots of tu-whit-tu-whoo animates
   little heart-shape faces of white.

These barn owls don't sleep
   in a fork of the trees
but in designer owl boxes
   that protect them from thieves.

Shy birds by day
   but when supper time calls
in silent flight they swoop for prey
   but oh those greedy screeches and snores.

The owlets hatch in April at different stages
   up to eight a pair have been encouraged on
they rid the land of small vermin so it's advantageous
   to count them among the friends of man.

And as I watch them winking and blinking
   saucer-eyes flashing like jewels
I wonder when looking back at us are they thinking
   just who are these silly owl fools!

Lucy Green

You Trusted Me

Springer, my companion, you were always there,
a mongrel with a difference, you were so aptly named
for your talent was to jump, four-footed, in the air,
with stiff-legged leap for which you were so famed.

But your gifts were many, you had a cunning nose,
for strangers, other dogs, and the hidden bone.
You could guard us with a vengeance, or be friendly if you chose
and welcome favoured visitors to the seclusion of your home.

You reigned in peace because you trusted me,
I was your servant, to give succour and to care,
even when your eyes so dimmed with age, you could barely see,
you always knew for certain I was there.

The years rushed by for you and age took hold,
with aches and pains never felt before,
no longer could you jump, your limbs were stiff and cold,
your eyes were blank, your tail thumped feebly on the floor.

I was your companion then, I was always there,
to whisper words of comfort, to bring a dish of tea,
until your sufferings were more than I could bear,
you relied on me for solace, because you trusted me.

Please forgive me, Springer, for that final act of mine,
when I sensed your weariness and your pain could see,
I called the vet in to halt the ravages of time,
because all I wanted was to set you free.

As you slowly drifted towards that peaceful land
in those final moments, did you close your eyes and see
a vision of the heavenly romping ground, before you licked my hand
in silent gratitude - because you trusted me.

Ann Rutherford

The Man And The Animal

Black Beauty! Silver! Rin Tin Tin! The March Hare!
Many more may be added, their fame to share.
In spite of our shortcomings we may honestly declare
That to a fairly high degree
Our love for animals is there.

Shall we agree that,
In the beginning man was made lord over all?
Like it or not, he answered the call,
But can he now feel proud and still stand tall
In the way he treats animals -
Wild and domesticated, large and small?

Animals are intelligent and will defend their own;
Their devotion to their owners will often have grown
To save a human being as they will save a calf
A pup or a mate, whichever it may be.
Where in a herd of wild horses will the stallion you see?

Which is more devoted, the horse or the dog -
And if the cat be included, Heaven forbid if not,
To its owner or companion, in the daily jog
Of life together, at work or at play, or resting on a log?

C A Knight

Dolly

A German shepherd through and through
My best mate is she!
Lots of walks
And lots of talks,
Follows me from room to room,
Even in the loo!
My love for her is so great -
Those big brown eyes
That knowing look,
When she gets a treat!
Her ball we play with when we can
Then by the fire at night we sit,
Gazing out to space
Thinking of the lovely day!
Hoping our friendship will never end
The bond between us is so great
Me and my old mate!

Kathleen Patricia Peebles

Bacon Saved

This is the tale of frivolous young pigs
Who smoked cigars when they gave up the cigs,
Because when they put on extra weight
Bacon and chops would have been their fate.

They were so obsessed in getting thinner
They exercised before their dinner,
In fact it made them pant and puff
As hammer and tongs was more than enough.

Paying a bit less tax was a good feel
And a cigar was smoked in place of a meal,
But someone said it was better after,
That in place of food was considerably dafter.

Their faces dropped as their weight went up
And they sobbed into a coffee cup.
Then their doctor said 'Give up all baccy,
Three small meals a day, give baccy the sacky.

Go to a gym, do not go for the burn,
Turn flab to muscle, go there to learn.
Get ready to give the mugger a bash
And invest wisely your hard-saved cash.'

M J Gilbert

Tommy

With your designer coat and air of hauteur,
who would ever glimpse the stray.
Who wandered in the yard one spring,
and liked us well enough to stay.

Camouflaged by marigolds,
Ginger tail curled tightly round.
Your eye took in each blade of grass,
your ear picked up each passing sound.

Your life filled up with sunny days,
when you would sit with glinting eye.
Jump up the wall two feet off ground,
to surprise a lazing fly.

Then came the day you nearly died,
the vet spelled out unspoken fears.
But anyway we took you home,
with faces smiling through our tears.

Something told us you'd pull through,
though recovery was long and hard.
You've come a long way from the scrap,
who wandered into our back yard.

Georgina Cook

Partners In Crime

Both adopted,
A roguish pair
Wherever there was trouble
You'd always find them there.
Belle - the dog, Saul - our son;
A dynamic duo, in search of fun.
He'd whisper secrets
In her big floppy ears.
She'd listen to his problems
And lick away the tears.
Saul's bedroom was supposed to be
Strictly a dog-free zone,
But, in spite of this, Belle could be found
At the side of his bed, with her bone.
They were both quite a handful,
But so eager to please,
Those partners in crime -
Our two adoptees.

Delia Dennett

Goldie

Fiendish feline eyes aglow
Upon a plant-pot poised
Blissfully ignorant of a foe
Glides he gracefully on
Round he goes, again and again
His fate, as crystal, clear
Shivery ripples encircle his den
'Tis all he ever has known

Sleek, confident, clad in black
Ever holding his glare
His prize will be the golden nugget
An honest win, fair and square

Water water all around
Alas the deed is done,
Floor is covered with shards of glass
Jewel-like in the sun

Pouncing on the great glass bubble
Where Goldie once had shone
Munching through his bones and scales
Our little friend has gone.

Asia

My Friend, The Cat

He scares the birds,
Eats the fish from their bowl,
My friend the cat
Is a funny old soul.
He's nervous and bewildered,
Yet resourceful and strong,
He's wild and fierce,
Yet loving and soft.
He sleeps all day.
He's out all night,
If he was human
This wouldn't be right.
And then there's the cleaning,
From his head to his toes,
The constant pruning
Of his silky, smooth coat.
He's a bit of a poser
And a bit of a clown,
But whenever I'm lonely
He's always around.
He brings a smile
Whenever I'm sad,
There is no other
Like my friend the cat.

Marvyn B Candler

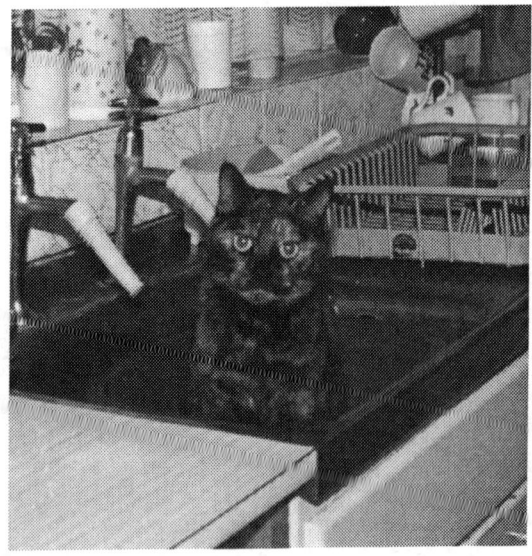

Charming Snake

Gently hissing, hiss, hiss
In warm scaly bliss

Slithering, slither, slither
Moving hither, thither

Loving, snug, happy my pet
Living colours, dry not wet

Yet beady eyed, beady eyed
Coiled in coils am I tied

His mouth open, open wide
Searching tongue side to side

See the fangs, such large fangs
Suffering from hunger pangs

No more can I write
Swallowed whole in one bite!

David A Watson

My Old Friend

I have a friend who's very old,
He has four legs and does as he's told.
He sleeps around in the house so free,
When I come in he follows me.

With four tanned legs and stature
So fine, I know he'll guard this house
Of mine. He likes to play and roll around,
And loves to bark and make a sound.

His favourite time is food of course,
He likes to eat as much as a horse.
After his feed he's raring to go, he sits
And waits beside the door.

A man's best friend for all to see,
But loved so much as a friend to me.

Richard Maddison

Fluff's Tale

As I snuggle down in my easy chair,
I remember those days long ago,
When I had ticks and fleas and greasy hair
And was smelly and not nice to know.
I wandered the street - a permanent roam -
And one or two people took pity
On this wretched beast that hadn't a home,
This poor little unwanted kitty.
One gave me meat and one gave me fish,
And I must say that this helped no end,
And one gave me milk in a pottery dish,
But I needed a much greater friend -
One who would take me under her wing
And provide a roof over my head.
Who would feed me, love me - everything -
And allow me to sleep on her bed!
So I came to live at 'twenty-one'
And was 'wined and dined' like a prince,
The comfort here is second to none,
And I have been here ever since.
Now people say 'What a beautiful cat!
You *must* enter him in a show,'
And I purr and secretly smile at that -
And remember those days long ago . . .

Anne Brown

Take Five

I think I'll take five minutes rest
Drink a cup of tea
Sit down and put my feet up
In front of the TV.

Just as I get settled
A sound comes to my ears
I stop and listen, oh no, yes
Confirming al my fears

Meow mee-oow
The cat's sitting at the door
The voice a semi-tone higher
The longer I ignore

The 'open up' summons has been given
I am commanded to obey
Confronted with a face that says
Well, why such a delay?

I've given up my tea's gone cold
The ironing must be done
We can't all have a cat's life
And lie sleeping in the sun!

Joan Cumming

Blind, Deaf - But Not Dumb.
The Old Cat At Twenty

Where does this howling come from?
Where's all this growling come from?
When you were young, you wouldn't dream
Of uttering such an anguished scream;
But now, in your sedate old age
You're like a lion in a cage!
And yet you've licked your bowl quite bare
And sit enthroned up on your chair.

   Then, as we watch you -
   Even as we touch you,

We hear you change your jungle howl
Into a soft, genteel meow.
You turn to us in great surprise,
Gazing about with shadowed eyes,
And with your usual feline poise
Disclaim all knowledge of that noise!

   But now we know:
   It's being *alone*
   That hurts you so!

Ruth Parker

Musky

Oh, Musky, why did you have to go,
My beloved pet, I did love you so,
For thirteen years you gave me love
But now you have gone to God above.
The love you gave will be with me always
Helping me through these very sad days.

I do know why you had to go
You were getting very tired, and so,
Our good Lord said, 'You've had enough,
So come Musky to me above.'

You have earned your rest, beloved pet,
A beautiful cat, I shall never forget.

I M Smith

I Am Cat

I can go anywhere
any table, any chair
in the window
on the ledge
I am cat
I have the edge
raid the cupboard
steal the cheese
I am cat
do as I please
I am cat
acrobatic yet serene
this house my castle
I am queen
the garden here
I roam alone
any intruder
escorted home
I expect my lunch
at the stroke of two
my pet humans?
I suppose they'll do

Wayne Cregan

Mischief

I let you think I was a stray
When I came to your house that very wet day
My pitiful cry, my look of plea
I liked you house and thought that's for me

You did not know I lived three doors away
But with them I did not want to stay
Noisy children who pulled me about
Your house looked so peaceful, I had no doubt

You tried to send me back when you found out
But I determine would not be cast out
I worried you till I had won
And then between you a solution done

Now with you contented am I
On my own cushion I sit or just lie
I like my own freedom to go as I please
But home I come peaceful and not to be teased

Upon your lap I sit and purr
Whilst with your hand you stroke my fur
Contented am I and forever will be
No more houses to check for me

This is my home and a new name
Lots of toys if I feel like a game
I think it quite right and very fitting
That my favourite game is the mistress knitting

My folks say there's only one name for me
So 'Mischief' it is and that's OK by me
I'll try to live up to my name's what I say
For mischief's my game by night or by day.

Joyce Boast

Thomas

Thomas is a strange cat
He has a real good home
He doesn't worry about that
He only wants to roam

In the doctor's waiting room
He went, where patients sat
They patted him, and stroked him
And said 'You lovely cat.'

He stands on edge of pavement
Looks to the left and right
Then carefully he crosses
With not a car in sight

At half past one, he makes his way
Up to the kitchen door
To see what scraps come his way
Some nice ones, he is sure

He dearly loves our summer house
Sits in a comfy chair
And sleeps, one night the door got shut
He spent the whole night there

Yes, Thomas is a strange cat
We love him just the same
And think one day his name should be
In the cat's hall of fame.

Doris Prowse

Four-Legged Friend

No answering back,
A plus when there's flack,

A listening ear,
A mop for a tear,

Unconditional cuddles,
No emotional muddles,

A great friend indeed,
Four legs on a lead,

There's 'sniffers' for drugs,
Those wonderful dugs!

Bright eyes for the blind,
Incredibly kind,

Guard dogs who protect,
With such an effect,

A great friend indeed,
Four legs on a lead.

Debra Neale

Solo The Kitten

We bought ourselves a Persian cat,
And Solo is her name.
As soon as we caught sight of her,
She set our hearts aflame.

She looks so sweet and cuddly,
She is so sweet and loving.
She watches us in all we do,
And follows everything moving.

As I sweep round with the vacuum,
She chases round the floor.
And when I switch it off again,
One look says let's have more.

She always has a tantrum,
When her food just doesn't suit,
But when she is so angry,
She looks so very cute.

As we leave for work each morning,
She looks as if to say.
I'll be all alone again,
For yet another day.

As we come home at lunchtime
She crawls out of her bed.
And as we put our coats back on,
Inclines her little head.

Why can't these humans be like me
Lie down and have a rest.
They are always rushing here and there,
My way of life is best.

Iris Covell

Sugar Plum Furry

I called my kitten Sugar Plum,
'Cos I like Tchaikovski's stuff
Shortened it to Sugar
As she was sweet enough,

Heard a shout from my other half -
'I'll kill that *bally* moggy'
The dead mouse in his slipper
Made him feel quite groggy!

Marion Lawson

Forever

They say there is no Heaven
For our well-beloved pets.
Do they not know such a thought
Brings sorrow and regrets?

But nature has a part to play
Throughout world's timeless age.
To birth, then fading, and renew
The seasons thus engage.

Moving creatures, hedgerow sounds
In the garden and in field.
The silent mysteries and power
Which all around us yield.

There is *no end* to anything
In nature's wondrous plans
No need to grieve, for all about
An earthly Heaven spans.

Sylvia Gorwill

Catisfying

I have a cat for company
Now that I am alone
It works both ways, don't you see
She reacts to the friendship shown
Love, food and warmth
Is all we need
To get along so well
She knows if I am feeling low
Although she cannot tell
Life has been much better
It is true, it is a fact
If you are feeling lonely
Then get yourself a cat.

Evelyn A Evans

My Cat

When I was 11 someone
brought me a cat.
It was furry and cuddly and
awfully fat.
With eyes of bright green and
a black coat that shines
red.
He's a marvellous companion
whilst lying in bed.

Smokey I called him,
he's a bundle of fun
he follows me all over
he thinks I'm his mum.
But I don't mind 'cos he's
quite a laugh except when
he's playing and gives a
good scratch.

Now I'm 13 and Smokey is
two, and I'm still his mum and
this is true, he still
follows me and his coat
still shines red.
And guess what? That's right
he still cuddles in bed.

Hayley Siddall (13)

The Naughty Dog

'Here, girl. Good girl.' Did she shout?
Does she want me to come?
'Oh. Come on, now. Time to leave.
Time to set off home.'
Not just yet, I've found a scent,
Got to investigate.
It's taking me across the field,
I hope that she can wait.

This scent is quite exciting,
It's winding here and there.
Wonder what's at the end of it,
Is it rabbit, is it hare?
I've found a bunny's burrow,
But it's too small to get inside.
And she'll be in such a temper,
Where am I going to hide.

'Where do you think you're going?
Just you come back here!'
She hasn't got a hope in hell,
While I'm on track, no fear.
'You wretched dog, just you wait
Till I catch up with you.
What makes you think you'll get away
With all the things you do?'

She's chased me right across the field,
And she is in a mood.
Must come up with something fast,
And it must be good.
I'll whimper, hold my paw up high,
Her anger melts away.
And this very naughty dog
Lives to hunt another day.

Maggie Moore

Lovely Kyley

She's brown and black
With big soft eyes
At times, I think, they almost talk
Please, take me for a walk!
She loves her home
loves the grass, her ball
her bone, rolling in the sun
She's lots of fun
for the children to play with
It wasn't always quite that way
For someone abandoned her
I'm sad to say!
She was nervous, and very timid
but a kindly vet, made her better
Gave her back, her spirit
A kindlier nurse brought her home
Now after tender loving care
No more will she roam
That kindly nurse, is her biggest fan
She's eight now, is Kyley
loved, happy, tail wagging 'pal'
Enjoys her walks, down the lane
doesn't even mind the rain
She knows, she's loved, every day
Ever since my daughter, the vet's nurse
gave her a home, that day
I hope she'll always, stay that way
soft loving Kyley.

Irene G Corbett

Sadie

With a wag of her tail and her cheeky grin,
She brings so much joy from within,
She lights up my life,
She gives me so much pleasure,
She really is a little treasure,
She is a very special lady,
My lovely mutt, my best pal Sadie.

Vannesa Fitzgerald

A Proper Charlie

I'm a King Charles Spaniel,
Named by Royal Decree,
Three hundred years of kingly choice,
I'm so proud to be me.
I try to be as regal as a King or Queen or Earl,
But then I see my favourite ball,
Thrown by my favourite girl.

We have such fun together,
I think I wear her out,
I'm never still, she's had her fill,
Of that I have no doubt.
But when we both feel weary,
I sit upon her knee,
She tugs my ears gently, I'm so happy to be me.

Although my forebears slumbered on a King's bed so I'm told
I would not swap my lovely girl,
For all King Charlie's gold . . .

Margaret W Farrand

Time For Walkies

It's time for walkies now mum,
Take me to the cliff or beach.
So I can have my run
And play in the sun.

The tide's out the beach is
Free it doesn't say 'no dogs please'.
Throw my ring so I can have a game,
Then bury it in the sand again.

As we walk along there are
Rock pools to splash in and out.
I'm getting wet but having fun
Shaking water all over mum.

Here comes another dog to
Join in our fun,
But I'm off to find my ring.
Now where did I bury it again?

The sea's coming in it
Keeps chasing me I chase it back.
But it doesn't give up, what am I to do?
It might swallow me up.

Come on Sandie you call
There won't be much beach
Left to play on soon.
Find your ring to bring home,
So we can play another sunny day.

Jenny Wiggins

ARRIVAL PRESS

Information

We hope you have enjoyed reading this book - and that you will continue to enjoy it in the coming years.

If you like reading and writing poetry drop us a line, or give us a call, and we'll send you a free information pack.

Write to :-   Arrival Press Information
1-2 Wainman Road
Woodston
Peterborough
PE2 7BU
(01733) 230762